In

Clintwood

BY OAKLEY DEAN BALDWIN

Copyright © 2018 ODB Publishing

Check out my other stories and books at:

http://thebaldwinstories.wix.com/author-blog

The following work is based mostly on family history, folklore, historical facts, court documents, tombstones, and newspaper articles.

Information was gathered from multiple sources and pieced together into a historical fiction story. As such, it should not be a definite source of information. Of course, after more than ninety years, stories are told and retold, with facts becoming harder to find. I am listing this story as fiction based on a true family story.

PROLOGUE

They say blood is thicker than water, but in most of the following stories you will learn that blood is not thicker than Moonshine. This spirituous fermented brew is sometimes known simply as "Shine" or "White Lightning." Some of these stories bring to light the deception and corruption over the lust and greed for control of these spirituous liquor concoctions. Along with many locations within our country, the attempts to control this alcoholic substance and the corruption it created was very strong throughout the 19th and early 20th centuries in the heart of small towns and communities. Areas in and around Pike, Floyd, and Letcher Counties in Kentucky were especially affected by moonshine production.

Counties such as Wise and Dickenson Counties were also highly concentrated areas for the strange brew in Virginia. These isolated areas are known as the Cumberland Mountain Range.

Times were hard in the Cumberland Mountain Range and on occasions there was a thin line between starving and making moonshine to get fast money to feed your family. For many folks it wasn't so much a moral issue as it was a survival issue. On the other hand, in this land since the 1600's moonshining has been passed down from generation to generation. Like a drug, once shining gets in your blood it can be very addictive and extremely hard to get out of your system. The problem is like enjoying a walk in the warm rain, white lightning can be just as deadly as lightning in a thunder storm.

Over time our laws have changed and products that were once legal become illegal and vice versa. Alcohol is one of these products that has this very shady history.

Use or consumption of alcohol in moderation is one thing, but it is another thing if consumption of alcohol becomes the catalyst for mayhem, abuse, violence and death. Like a plague or a wildfire you have laws in effect to maintain control of it. This is why the Government in 1919 stepped in and tried to gain control of its production through the Prohibition Laws.

The Prohibition Laws were doomed from the start. Everyone knows you can't control white lightning anymore then you can control lightning in a thunder storm.

So the Government, in way over their heads, got in the alcohol control business and simply started selling it. Questionably the old adages, if you can't beat them, join them. This appears to be the governments take over attitude.

On a side note, the youngest county in this group is Dickenson County. It was formed in 1880 from parts of Buchanan, Russell, and Wise Counties. It is named after my 1st cousin 6x removed William Jennings Dickenson; a delegate to the Virginia General Assembly from Russell County, 1859–1861, 1865–1867, and 1877–1882.

Dickenson County is often called "Virginia's Baby." The county consists of three towns, Clintwood, Haysi and Clinchco.

PART ONE
POUND GAP

Before we start with the factual account of one of these tragic incidents, let me discuss the main focus point of this book, which is the shootout between Sheriff Claudius Pridemore Fleming and Special Agent James Sherman Mullins of the Virginia Department of Prohibition Enforcement. This shootout was an extremely grievous incident which occurred on the front steps to the Dickenson County Courthouse, in Virginia on August 6th, 1926.

The spark that ignited this deadly encounter was initiated by the sale and consumption of "Moonshine."

I need to give you some background information as to the cultural, social, and political tides that were flowing in the country at that time in history for this story. One can only ponder the real importance of it all at the time.

As you will soon learn the State of Virginia based a life changing decision on the relevance of the Pound Gap story and the relationship between Sheriff Claudius Pridemore Fleming and Special Agent James Sherman Mullins. Both of these men are my 3rd cousins.

Let's venture back in time from the date of the Dickenson County shootout on August 6th, 1926 to the Pound Gap Massacre on May 14th, 1892.

The Pound Gap Massacre happened and unfolded at the border lines of Kentucky and Virginia in the county of Wise, Virginia.

This massacre involved several of the Mullins and Fleming family members as well as involving the infamous Marshall Benton "Doc" Taylor. AKA (Red Fox Taylor).

Both James Sherman Mullins and Claudius Pridemore Fleming would have learned about the Pound Gap Massacre from their kinfolk probably many times over as family folklore and bed time stories. Claudius Pridemore Fleming was raised in Wise County and was related to the Fleming brothers who also just happened to be suspects in that Pound Gap massacre.

James Sherman Mullins was related to Ira (Bad Ira) Mullins and several other family members that had been massacred at the Pound Gap that fateful day of May 14th, 1892.

Both men would have been told this story many times over throughout childhood and even into adulthood. I'm sure the family gatherings were abuzz with the gossip, both old and new, concerning these incidents. The stories they heard were unique to each of the family's history, of course that is depending on which family was doing the re-telling of it.

This shooting incident was big news in 1892; it was reported as far away as Washington, D.C. by the Washington Post and in New York by The National Police Gazette Newspaper.

James Sherman Mullins would have been twenty-five years old at the time of the Pound Gap Massacre. Claudius Pridemore Fleming would have been about fourteen.

When you get time, you can read all about this family story of the Pound Gap Massacre in our eBook / Paperback book "Killing Moonshine Mullins." One of the most exciting stories ever told.

PART TWO

BAD BLOOD

Sometimes too much of a good thing is not good for you. Moonshine is like any other mind influencing substance. Too much moonshine is definitely not good for you.

Back then, whoever controlled the moonshine business controlled the money and had influence with many Law Enforcement Officers. Let's face it; some Law Enforcement Officers were on the take. At the turn of the 20th century in southeastern Kentucky and western Virginia along with John "Devil John" Wright, the Mullins and Fleming families had control on the moonshining operations in much of the Cumberland Mountain Range.

Moreover, they were all related by one way or another. What could possibly go wrong? One of the young impressionable Fleming boys was King Solomon "Bad Sol" Fleming, referred to simply as Sol Fleming from here forward. He was the son of John Jefferson Fleming and Mary (Johnson) Fleming.

Sol Fleming began running with his uncle John "Devil John" Wright at the age of about seventeen. John was the law but he was also a "Regulator," which meant through fear and intimidation he could pretty much do about anything he wanted to do. Rumors had it that the Regulators were a splinter group of the Clansmen. Some say they were, some say they weren't. Either way, their tactics were not any different than gangs or organized criminal behavior that has gone on since the beginning of time.

At Boone Creek, in Letcher County Kentucky, in November 1900, a shocking double homicide occurred during an attempt to intimidate a local widower and her son. Sol Fleming, his brother Elijah, and a hand full of Regulators murdered widow Jemima (Blankenship) Hall along with her nineteen year old son Sherwood Hall.

We are not exactly sure what caused these murders, but many believe it was to obtain Jemima Hall's property. Jemima had married a much older man named James Allen Hall, he was the property owner. James had died earlier in the same year and left his estate and property to Jemima.

On a side note, I find it very odd that just a few weeks after these murders on December 6th, 1900, John "Devil John" Wright signed the Administrative Bond and had his name added as one of the administrators of Jemima Hall's (the deceased) Estate.

Boot tracks in the mud at the crime scene led to the arrest of one of the murderers. The evidence collected included the obvious appearance of one of the boot tracks as assessed by the detectives, indicating there had been a repair made to that boot by being patched with a different piece of leather.

Sure enough, one of the suspects, Elijah Fleming, was questioned and during his questioning they noticed one of his boots had a leather patch in the exact location as the boot prints at the crime scene. This evidence was a dead giveaway of his participation in the murders.

Once he was presented with this evidence he confessed and gave up the names of all the other men involved. You might say he sang like a bird the story of murder most foul.

In 1901, many of these murderers were tracked down and arrested. Sol Fleming wasn't going to give up and go peacefully. Once the officers caught up with him, he engaged in a shootout with the detectives and was wounded in the hip during his arrest. He was wounded so badly he had no choice but to give up. Sol was held in the Whitesburg Jail. Several of the Regulators that were still at large started communicating threats even to the Judge.

Because of threats to the Judge and Courthouse a change of incarceration facility was initiated and Sol was moved temporarily to Stanford Jail in Lincoln County, Kentucky.

In 1901, Sol Fleming was sent back to Letcher County and was found to be guilty of murder and sent away to prison.

After a short stay in prison, sometime before 1907 with good behavior Sol was pardoned by Governor John C.W. Beckham and released from prison. As you will soon learn letting "Bad Sol" out of prison for good behavior was a big mistake. It was like placing a fox in the hen house. You could say when Sol was good he was good, but when he was bad he was bitter. Pun intended!

PART THREE
LAW CHAOS & TURMOIL

Letcher, Pike and Floyd Counties all share geographical land boarders. This chapter proves just how difficult it was at times to be in the Law Enforcement profession in these counties.

The following stories are examples of some of the obstacles and challenges Lawman had to overcome.

In the year 1910, William G. Dunehoo was elected Sheriff of Floyd County, Kentucky. He had previously been elected Sheriff of Floyd County from 1902 through 1904. It is not known why he was not re-elected after he left office in 1904.

In 1912, he was re-elected Sheriff. In 1914, the primary election turned into chaos and moonshine was at the center of politics. Sheriff Dunehoo was running for re-election for another two year term. This re-election campaign he had two other men interested in his job as High Sheriff. A man named Joe. R. Barron and a Floyd County Deputy Sheriff named George Wash Smith.

Directly before the primary election, Sheriff Donehoo assigned Deputy Sheriff George Wash Smith to pick up a prisoner from Virginia. Once he arrived back to Floyd County with the prisoner, Sheriff Donehoo assigned him another prisoner to pick up. He must have been a little worried about his competition. This time the trip would take him out of state to Fort Wayne Indiana, which would keep him away from Floyd County for several days past the primary election.

Deputy Sheriff George Wash Smith saw this assignment as a convenient way to keep him out of town and out of the county long enough so he could not effectively campaign for High Sheriff. Out of sight, out of mind, especially to the voters.

Campaigning for office was a face to face interaction back then. There was no social media other than your local weekly newspaper and Church meetings.

In response to his new out of state assignment and before he started his trip, George Wash Smith had post cards sent out to the citizens of Floyd County with his campaign promises.

These post cards would soon cause a reprimand which turned into violence. The cards stated the following information:

The Card was dated:

"April 27, 1914

To the voters of Floyd County

Sir,

Having just returned from Virginia with a prisoner, and acting under orders of the sheriff, I am again on my way to Fort Wayne, Ind, for a prisoner, I won't be able to see you before the election. Kindly remember me and my ticket on next Tuesday and make our majority as big as possible.

Promising you in return a good, clean, sober administration, I am yours truly, Wash Smith."

Sheriff Donehoo took high offence to this post card because of the reference to promising a good, clean and sober administration. He felt the message on this card insinuated that his character was not good, clean and / or sober.

On Monday, April 27th, 1914, on the eve of the primary election, Sheriff Dunehoo and his son Henry paid a visit to the Floyd County Courthouse.

Henry, who was his father's driver, was sitting on the stone wall outside of the courthouse waiting for him to finish some business. Once this business was completed, they left the courthouse and stopped by the jail across the street to deliver some jail bond information to one of the prisoners.

Traveling at a very fast pace, Deputy George Wash Smith had just returned early from picking up his out of state prisoner and was at the jail using the phone.

It was the end of the work day and Dunehoo had already started drinking alcohol in the libations of the spirits of between seventy to one hundred proofs. It wasn't long before Dunehoo saw George Wash Smith and he wasted no time in letting the accusations began to fly about the post card George had sent out and he proceeded to accuse Smith of hitting him "below the belt" with questioning his character. It seems he and George shared different versions as to the personal definitions of "Character".

Dunehoo became very upset; getting himself all worked up, fueled by the firewater in his flask.

Dunehoo questioned the implication that he had sent Smith for the prisoners to keep him from campaigning. Dunehoo then began to question the "sober" statement in the post card and called Smith a hypocrite.

The confrontation quickly escalated and Dunehoo began cursing and yelling at Smith. They went full steam into a heated argument which led to an altercation. At this point Smith had heard enough, he got angry and punched Dunehoo in the face. They both went down to the ground, with Smith on top of Sheriff Dunehoo.

Henry Dunehoo was alerted after hearing his father yelling and came running into the jail. He saw Smith on top of his father beating him with his fists. Henry began hitting Smith on his back and on the back of his head.

Henry's actions caused Smith to get off of his father. Smith then ran out the back door of the jail. Henry pulled two pistols and began to chase after Smith, using a gun in each hand to pummel Smith as he attempted to make his escape. Somehow Smith had lost his pistol in the fracas with Sheriff Dunehoo during their rolling around on the ground.

Smith finally made his way to the back gate of the jail property; he pulled the gate shut behind himself, he held it closed attempting to keep Henry off of him.

After a few seconds Sheriff Dunehoo had recovered and arrived at the gate. He was so upset and intoxicated he pulled his revolver and shot a round through the fence. When he could not get the gate open he shot through the gate that George Smith was holding hitting Smith directly in the stomach.

The wounded Smith picked up a board from the broken fence and opened the gate and began to beat Dunehoo over the head with the board. Because of this beating Dunehoo fell to the ground, George Smith jumped back on him and when he did, Henry then put a gun to Smith's head, saying "I'll kill you if you don't get off of my father."

George Smith backed off again, and when he did Donehoo jumped back on Smith. Deputy Barron and some others arrived about that time and began to pull the two men apart and restored some order to the scene.

Smith was taken to the local Hospital and immediately operated on. The local paper reported news of his health over the next few days. His deathbed testimony was taken in case he did not survive his wound.

Fortunately, he did not develop infection from his wound and lived to testify. After many delays, the trial was held in November of 1914. Judge Moses Wright excused himself and Judge A.W. Fite of the Cherokee Circuit sat on the bench. The Coroner, John W. Miller, was responsible for the many jurors and witnesses.

Because both men were so well known in Floyd County it took a pool of three hundred forty six jurors to select twelve people that were qualified and impartial.

The Rome Tribune Herald Newspaper dated Sunday, November 8th, 1914 stated: "Sheriff Dunehoo found guilty of shooting another; fined $1,000.00. "

Sheriff Dunehoo had already withdrawn from the primary election of April 28th, 1914, and Joe R. Barron won the three man race. Technically, Dunehoo was still sheriff of Floyd County until January 1st, 1915 and was still responsible for running the jail and the courts, with the exception of his own trial. George Wash Smith continued in law enforcement and went on to win the sheriff's election on April 6th, 1916 for one term.

It was reported that Joe R. Barron won the race because of the actions and turmoil of the other two men. During this time of chaos and turmoil in the Floyd County Sheriff's Department, through back door politics Solomon "Bad Sol" Fleming became a Floyd County Deputy Sheriff. Somehow the background information was missed that Sol Fleming had previously been in prison for murder.

And unfortunately, there was no reform to his behavior; it was not too long before "Bad Sol" was in big trouble again.

Apparently, it wasn't long before Sol had gotten into some trouble in the community of Beaver and his job as Deputy Sheriff was in jeopardy.

On September 4th, 1915 Pike County Constable Sidney Tackett was sitting on the front porch of his cousin, Will Tackett's home in the community of Weeksbury, in Floyd County.

Sidney, known as "Sid" came over to Floyd County. He had a warrant for the arrest of Mr. Louis Cook and was searching for him. Word got to Sol that Sid Tackett was in his county and it didn't take him long to go pay him a visit.

Deputy Sheriff Sol Fleming rode up on his horse to the front gate of Will Tackett's home. He called over to Sid and said he wanted to talk and asked Will Tackett to come and hear them.

    Sol dismounted his horse keeping a hold on the reins. They walked down the dirt road some distances talking.

    Nothing wrong with a peaceful walk on a beautiful day, but it didn't take long for the talk to turn ugly. Out of the blue and for no reason, from the tone of his voice Sid could hear and read the body language that Sol was becoming very upset. He could sense the tension in the air. Hairs standing straight on his arms and neck, he knew it was becoming a dangerous situation, unfolding in front of him. Trouble was brewing like a bubbling cauldron. It was about to boil over.

Sol was becoming so upset it concerned Sid to the point that he put his hand on the handle of his pistol and told Sol, "I do not want any trouble with you; I have always treated you right."

Then Sol said to Sid, "You and Squire Tackett had falsely prosecuted me." "I have never prosecuted you in none of your cases." replied Sid. Then Sol told Sid, "Take your hand off of your pistol." Sol said, "I heard you, Pharoh and Willie Johnson said you were going to mob me up next time you caught me out."

"I have never heard tell of it, I do not want to hurt you. If I did I would hurt you here but do not want any trouble with any one." answered Sid. Tensions were high; Sid would not take his hand off his pistol.

Sol then accused Sid of taking his hand cuffs. Sid reminded Sol that he had offered money for the set of hand cuffs and he wouldn't take any money for them.

Sol then eyed Sid's pistol and nodded his head towards it, stating, "I got the right to take it off of you. I believe I will just summons Uncle Will there to take it off of you." Will Tackett overheard what Sol had said. Disagreeing, Will spoke up and said, "No, you will not do that, you and him are both good men, settle up fair and don't have any trouble."

Unbeknownst to Sid or Uncle Will, Sol did not come alone, while they were talking; he was walking Sid down the creek toward where Sol's comrade Solomon Johnson was hiding. Sol was walking Sid and Uncle Will into an ambush situation.

Once they got close to where Johnson was hiding, Sol pulled out his pistol and shot Sid in the right arm.

Sol backed up some and from behind a loom brush Solomon Johnson starting shooting at Sid and Uncle Will. Already wounded, Sid dropped to his knees and returned fire with his left hand striking Johnson in the legs. Johnson fired between eight and ten rounds at them before Sid wounded him.

We are not sure if this was a trap or setup but it sure smells like one. They say the shot to Sid's right arm nearly took his arm off. Sol then helped Solomon Johnson get to his horse and they both left the scene.

It was two days later on September 6th, when Sol was arrested for malicious assault. He bonded out of jail that day and left for home. This assault charge was upgraded to murder on Friday September 10th, 1915, when Sid Tackett died from blood poisoning caused by the shot from Sol's gun. Would Sid Tackett have lived a full life had Sol not been released and pardoned from prison by Governor Beckham?

Floyd County Sheriff Joe R. Barron assigned Deputy Sheriff Willie Hall to arrest Sol for murder. He arrested Sol and led him down to the train station to catch the Big Sandy Train headed to Prestonsburg, Kentucky. Before the train could pull out of the station, about a dozen heavily armed men surrounded them. One man stated he was a Pike County Deputy which demanded the immediate surrender of Sol Fleming.

About the time the train engineer began to ring the "all abroad" bell, two of these armed men pointed their rifles at the engineer and told him, "the train must stand still."

Witnesses sitting in their seats aboard the train watched out of the windows as the drama unfolded. Several rather interesting controversies among the armed men and deputies arose as to conflicting jurisdiction between which county court would hear the case. Pike County or Floyd County? There's nothing like a little confusion over who's in charge when there's a group of armed men surrounding the train with the passengers in the middle. A reasonable conclusion in light of the circumstances would normally come down to which side has the most guns.

Floyd County won the disagreement if there is a winning aspect to this kind of predicament and the trial was held in Prestonsburg, Kentucky in Floyd County. During the trial evidence showed Sol Fleming had no reason or warrant to arrest Sid Tackett. He was found guilty and sentenced to life in Frankfort, Kentucky Reformatory. In some cases reformatory just doesn't do justice to real life situations, it's an oxymoron for prison. In October 1917, Sol was transferred to the reformatory. Sol was a good carpenter and worked for about five years in the mail room. He once again gained the trust of the prison officials and had some freedoms within the prison.

In November of 1923, prison officials received word that Sol's mother was very ill and was about to die.

Because of his good behavior in prison he was granted leave and allowed under armed guard to visit his mother at her home in Longfork, Kentucky.

Once they arrived near night fall, Sol told his guard that if he wanted to live to see the sun raise he better leave Longfork tonight. It was good advice but now it is called "communicating a threat." Being isolated so far back in the woods this threat scared the guard so bad that he left that night fearing for his own safety.

Sol did not voluntarily return to the prison after his mother's funeral. He was now considered an escaped fugitive. The state soon placed a $600 reward for his capture and return to the Kentucky Reformatory.

He hid out for a while but it wasn't long before Sol was back in more trouble. It seems trouble came looking for Sol again. He got involved in a family feud between his brothers George and Morgan and a sister-in-law Adeline (Bentley) Fleming.

Adeline had gone back to the Bentley home to get away from George Fleming. Sol convinced her to come see George because he was injured and needed her. Adeline agreed and started out with Sol, but in short time she changed her mind about going to see George. She wanted to go back to her parents' home and got into an argument with Sol about changing her mind. Further encounters with trouble at this point could have been avoided if Sol would have remembered that a woman's right to change her mind is her 1st prerogative.

Stubbornly, Sol was not going to allow her to change her mind and ended up shooting her twice before she could escape from him. She did escape and was able to make her way back to her family even though she was seriously wounded.

Once this argument and shooting was reported to her family two of her brothers, Roosevelt and Simon Bentley went looking for Sol. The brothers hid out and waited for Sol, whatever it took, they were not going to let Sol get away with his shooting of an unarmed woman. It wasn't long before they caught up to him as he was attempting to leave town but they cut him off at the pass. For over two years, Sol had been an escapee, a free man until January 5th, 1925. A gun battle broke loose over the distance of a quarter of a mile between Sol and the Bentley brothers.

Over sixty shots were fired during the shootout. Sol Fleming had been shot several times but he wasn't giving up. After some period of time Sol's gun fell silent.

The Bentley brothers cautiously approached him. There was Sol, lying on the ground silent; it had taken twelve rounds to bring him down. Sol succumbed to his wounds and slipped out into eternity.

MORE TURMOIL

Letcher County Deputy Constable Joel Martin "Mart" Wright was shot on August 4th, 1916 while making an arrest of a moonshiner.

Charlie Hazen had a dry goods store in the community of Neon. He was at home when Deputy Constable Wright approached him with a warrant for his arrest. Charlie started to resist arrest and Wright pulled his pearl handled 38 caliber pistol out and struck him over the head. When he hit Charlie his pistol flew out of his hand onto the ground. Then Charlie Hazen's daughter, fourteen year old Mary Hazen quickly ran up to him and picked it from the ground. She turned the pistol on Deputy Joel Wright and shot him in the shoulder.

This shot deflected downwards through his lung and severed his spinal cord dropping him on the spot. Mary and her father were both arrested by other officers.

Deputy Constable Wright was taken to the Good Samaritan Hospital in Lexington, Kentucky. Doctors treated him the best they could. They informed him that his wound was fatal and released him to spend his last days with his family. Twenty days later on August 24th, 1916 he died from his wound.

Deputy Constable Wright was survived by his wife Mary Alice (Killen) Wright. He is buried in Potter Cemetery, also known at Murdered Man's Cemetery in Jenkins, Letcher County, Kentucky. It is said there are more than twenty murder victims buried in this Cemetery.

On July 25th, 1918, Dickenson County thirty-eight year old Deputy Andrew Jefferson "Jeff" Long was shot and killed from ambush near the community of Trammel by three men. These three men were seeking revenge following an earlier raid by Deputy Long on their moonshine still and operation.

The first sign of trouble was when the crew of a Carolina, Clinchfield, and Ohio Railroad train spotted a rider-less horse meandering and walking along the railroad tracks. The train crewmen made a request to the conductor to stop the train.

The conductor recognized the horse as belonging to Dickenson County Deputy Long. He instructed his crew to begin a search for Deputy Long.

It wasn't just a few minutes before Deputy Long's body was discovered on the road just a short distance from the railroad tracks. The train conductor notified local law enforcement of their shockingly horrific discovery.

Evidence at the crime scene during the investigation revealed that three men had setup an ambush the previous night and waited for Deputy Long to pass by them in the morning. Apparently, Deputy Long had developed a routine of coming to work about the same time on the same road. In law enforcement, becoming routine in your traveling habits will always end poorly.

It is believed that the men ambushed him with shotguns as the result of a previous raid that Deputy Long had been a participant in.

All three men were rounded up and arrested. At trial all three men were found guilty of murder and were sentenced to life in prison. Deputy Long was survived by his wife Anna Mariah (Phillips) Long and ten children.

PART FOUR
PROHIBITION

      Prohibition arrives and so does an Agent; a law man attempting to eradicate the well-hidden moonshine stills. The Officer sometimes fights as he attempts to enforce justice and uncover the truth behind corruption in his community. The federal government began taxing liquor in the 1860's to help fund the Union side of the Civil War effort. At the end of the war congress kept the tax and thus the selling of moonshine black market took off.

      On October 28th, 1919, the Government ratified the Eighteenth Amendment to the U.S. Constitution. This amendment was known as the Prohibition Amendment. It prohibited the manufacture, sale, transportation, import, and export of intoxicating liquors.

This amendment provided an even greater demand for liquor and reaped greater rewards for those who engaged in moonshining and bootlegging. One would have to ask themselves if this amendment would ever justify the loss of life over the fourteen years of its existence (1919-1933). Sometimes greed, the second of the seven deadly sins, controls the mind of everyone.

Drinking bad bootleg whiskey also resulted in many deaths. Poisoning from lethal rubbing alcohol, paint thinners, and antifreeze were a few of the contaminants used that caused illnesses due to increased production demands. Moonshining stills started growing like wild fire. The stills grew so fast that there weren't enough federal or state agents to put the fires out. The flow of illegal liquor got so out of hand that the government basically declared war on moonshiners.

Federal and State budgets for new agents were very tight. Many parts of the country had one agent attempting to cover four or five counties. Early on in this inception the situation favored the moonshiners, along with plenty of supplies like grain, yeast, sugar and corn.

After about two years the government started to find its footing. Agents followed the trail from the large purchases of the materials to make the mash from the store directly to the still sites.

Some agent's sense of smell got really keen at smelling fermenting mash from miles away. These were the moonshine mash connoisseurs. Like a blood hound they could follow the wind leading them back to the mash.

Once supplies got hard to get, many moonshiners began fighting among themselves, stealing supplies, mash, equipment etc. Some moonshiners would even share with federal and local law enforcement officers the actual locations and hiding places of other moonshiner's stills, personally stomping out the competition. All's fair in love, war, and moonshine or so it is said.

PART FIVE

LOOSE LIPS

One such "sharing of location" incident happened in the adjoining county of Wise. A stranger and drifter named George Tilman showed up in the Indian Creek and Gilliam Hollow communities. He claimed to be an escaped convict from the state of Texas.

After bouts of humor and strong drinks it didn't take him long before he worked his way into the fold as one of the good old boys. The group that he was now associated with was known for making the best liquor. No nasty headache and no next day hang-over. This large outfit was made up of the families of Mullins, Gilliams, Addingtons, Blairs, Meades, and the Branhams.

Word got out that they always made the best and highest proofed liquor. It wasn't long before the big players from surrounding counties and states made their investments in this liquid gold.

Business grew so fast that this group could not keep enough supplies on hand to make the mash. They contracted with out of state wholesale companies to ship their supplies, corn, malt, sugar, and etc. by train to the town of Norton, Virginia. These box cars were always unloaded at breakneck speed during nighttime to use the darkness for cover.

The demand was so large for moonshine they resorted to purchasing one hundred pound bags of supplies catching the eyes of the Baldwin-Felts Detectives and other law enforcement officers.

Soon arrests would be forthcoming; law enforcement officers sat on the load undercover and waited for their moonshiners return. Those arrested started the trouble among the moonshiners. Big money, jealousy and suspicious minds were now looking warily into the eyes of each moonshiner.

Paranoid with suspicion of each other, hard feelings and quarrels continued. George Tilman had a gut feeling; he decided it was time to disappear and get out of town. He demanded his share of the last run and a portion of the hidden moonshine. After a volley of threats back and forth between George and Willie Addington the group agreed to give George six five-gallon buckets of moonshine and his part of the cash from the last run.

George told the group that he was headed back to Texas. At least this is what he wanted them to think he was going to do. The temptation of quick cash had overcome George so he decided to hide his moonshine in the weeds near a small frog pond. He needed some time to let tempers cool down and hoped they would forget about him. He left town and went into hiding.

All the time his plan was to notify the law about the location of the large Mullins and Addington Stills. Just a few weeks later, George mailed a letter to the law in Wise County notifying them of the still location. A few days later a swarm of law enforcement officers raided the site of the large still capturing most of the moonshiners in the act of making shine, caught red handed you might say.

Agents and Officers destroyed the stills and arrested all of the men involved. Somehow the word got out that George Tilman wrote the letter to the law telling them about the illegal operations. Now they wanted revenge on George. The moonshiners searched for George and his buckets of moonshine for months to no avail.

One day several months later, a small group of young boys gigging frogs, came across George Tilman's hidden moonshine buckets in the weeds. The boys directly told their parents, who then told the area moonshiners. One thing they knew for sure is that one day George Tilman would come back for his shine.

They wanted revenge and took turns watching the hidden buckets of moonshine, night after night.

Stealthy watching and waiting, weeks went by without so much as a sighting.

Then, in September George was spotted on the train coming into the town of Norton, Virginia. The State Fair was about to start and they suspected that George would come get his shine to sale at the Fair to thirsty customers.

If he showed up to get his shine their plan was to beat him, rob him of his money and clothes, and then turn him loose naked.

After a few more nights of watching they guessed right. Up the creek came George slowly creeping, he had finally returned for his hidden moonshine.

George should have had a belly full of fear with a nauseating sense of danger. Greed must have overwhelmed his innate sense of fear.

Vigilante dark eyes followed him with a glance of contempt. He walked directly into their trap and right into their arms. This trip up the creek turned out to be a deadly adventure for George. He was literally up the creek without a paddle. The vigilante group of men jumped out from behind the bushes and grabbed him; George's face turned as pale as death.

Before George could engage them in debate they tied his hands behind his back and placed a red bandanna handkerchief round his mouth gagging him in the process.

They walked him up to a bridge. There they stood overshadowed by old trees. These trees had been bordered at one time by high hedges. The size of the trees and the outspreading extent of their boughs cast a gloomy shadow over the scene even when the sun was at its highest.

The sinister plan to beat and rob him quickly changed to horror. One of the men in the group was Willie Addington. Quick to the point, he scowled "Beating him up ain't enough for this double-crossing SOB, I'm going to kill the dirty bastard."

Willie's dark eyes glistened like black coal flakes, without further warning Willie pulled his revolver from his belt and fired point blank hitting Tilman in his chest.

George then fell to the ground struggling for his breath. As he was writhing on the ground the gag came out of his mouth. The bullet had pierced his lung. Bleeding from the mouth he could hardly cry for help. He suddenly suffocated and drowned in his own blood.

The other men in the group were stricken and paralyzed with fear. They encircled the body, removed his clothing and pushed his dead corpse off of the bridge down the embankment.

His naked body was discovered the next day and reported to the High Sheriff. The Sheriff could not find one witness that had any information about this murder.

Several kind hearted local folks made his wooden casket and dug his grave. They couldn't even find a preacher to perform the service for George. One of the local men said a prayer over his grave as it was being covered. The investigation into the killing of George Tilman went unsolved.

Because of these types of horrifying incidents and other unsolved crimes over a two year period, four-thousand agents were hired across the country and many worked overtime to combat the rising flood of moonshine.

At the time Dickenson County, Virginia was not one of these counties covered by these agents and things there were just getting worse.

PART SIX
CRY FOR ASSISTANCE

The Honorable John R. Saunders, Attorney-General of the Commonwealth of Virginia was responsible for appointing and assigning new Prohibition Agents in the state of Virginia.

He received a letter dated December 23, 1923 from Claude F. Beverly the Commonwealth of Virginia, Department of Game and Inland Fisheries Supervisor of the 9th District which included Dickenson County. Even though Claude F. Beverly did not have the control of illegal alcohol under his direct authority as a Game and Inland Fisheries Supervisor; he knew firsthand how appalling and unacceptable the lack of law enforcement was becoming in Dickenson County.

This letter explains the lawless conditions in 1923 in Dickenson County Virginia. It goes as follows:

"Dear Mr. Saunders: Conditions, so far as the prohibition laws are concerned, are simply appalling in this (Dickenson) county. The law is simply being trampled underfoot on every side and moonshining and bootlegging is notoriously open and flagrant, not only in the out-of-the-way places, but right in the county-seat of the county.

Disregard for this law is, naturally, breeding disregard for all other laws. Consequently, perjury is just winked at and sanctioned.

And if conditions continue to grow worse in this county, it will not be long until anarchy reigns and the county will be in worse shape than Mexico ever was.

I am not exaggerating this matter in the least; I am simply telling the God's naked truth, and I cannot paint it nearly as bad as it really is. The prohibition question has been made a football of politics by Federal, county and local authorities in the county until each is afraid to make a move for fear of losing a vote.

Of all the counties of Southwest Virginia that I travel over, none are in such shape as Dickenson. I wonder if there is any way in the world to better conditions. I would be very glad if you would mention this matter to Mr. Fuliwler, the Federal Prohibition Director and tell him that the county is simply overrun with violators and that criminals of every stripe are now drifting into this county from Kentucky, attracted by the easy picking they find here.

Perhaps Mr. Fulwiler might bring some force to bear to remedy conditions. In this connection, I must ask you to please not mention my name in connection with this report, for the very good reason that the man who lives among them and who is even suspected of reporting them is a marked man for all time, and , sooner or later, he will fare badly at their hands.

I read the speech of ex-Governor Henry J. Allen, of Kansas, at the prohibition conference, held at Washington some time ago, in which he said, among other striking things, that if he was Governor of any state in which there was any county or community that did not obey the law, that, that community would go to sleep at night to the sound of taps and wake at morning to the reveille of drums.

I thought at the time Dickenson County would be the first place in Virginia he would strike at if he was Governor of this Commonwealth. I hope you may aid the law-abiding citizens of this county in some way. And I trust you will regard this letter as confidential, so far as I am concerned.

I would like to speak out boldly and fearlessly, but for the present I prefer the hills and dales of Dickenson to the shores of Eden. We elected a very fine young man Commonwealth's Attorney at the recent election. He is a dry man in every sense of the word and will be glad to do all in his power to help remedy conditions. He simply slid in between two professed wets, wet personally and otherwise.

We hope Mr. Whitehead can be at the March term of our court to assist Mr. Sutherland (E.J.) in getting started out right. With very best wishes,

I am Your Friend,

Claude F. Beverly."

E.J. Sutherland was Elihu Jasper Sutherland. He was also known as "Li" to his friends and family.

Anguished cries like this letter and these types of complaints helped to propel the need for a prohibition agent in Dickenson County. Claude F. Beverly had good reason to worry about his safety; the Dickenson County Justice of the Peace obtained warrants on several men for being drunk and breaking out the windows at the school building. Within a few days his home was burned to the ground.

On September 16th, 1923, John Hatfield, cousin of "Devil Anse" Hatfield of the feud fame and Steve Wood, murdered Erwin Mullins in Sandlick, Dickenson County.

John, Steve, and Erwin were all working together on a large moonshining operation. It is not known what the reason was behind the assault, but some believe John and Steve started to suspect Erwin of snitching on them to the law.

They struck Erwin in the head with a blunt object fracturing his skull; they then pushed him over a cliff off the side of the mountain. His body was found at the bottom of the cliff several days later by family members.

John Hatfield and Steve Wood were arrested for the murder of Erwin Mullins and stood trial in the Circuit Court of Dickenson County. Both men were found guilty of first degree murder and sentenced to twenty years in prison. They were sent to the Wise County Jail for safe keeping.

Within days they were free again, both men and three others broke out of the Wise County jail. They broke out the bars from the jail window to obtain their freedom.

Sheriff A.L.P. Corder of Wise County immediately formed a posse of forty men. They scoured and searched the hills and mountains in the surrounding area until they located them.

Once surrounded Steve Wood immediately surrendered. John being a career criminal did not give up and was taken by force. He was still nursing his injuries during his transportation to the Virginia State penitentiary.

Erwin Mullins was married to Mecie (Butcher) Mullins. They had three young children and Mecie was expecting their forth when he was murdered.

Prohibition Agent for Dickenson

James Sherman Mullins was born July 28^{th,} 1867. He was the son of Isaac and Elizabeth Mullins. In 1902 James was appointed U.S. Deputy Marshall in Southern Virginia. In 1922 and 1923 James served as Justice of the Peace in Dickenson County. During this time of service James had broken up over fifty moonshine stills.

James Sherman Mullins was tall and slender; his countenance was reserved and pensive. He had dark hair and dark eyes. He was known to be honest and dry. Dry as to mean he did not get drunk.

Because of his reputation to be honest and dry James Mullins was the appointed Agent with the Virginia Department of Prohibition Enforcement on March 10th, 1924.

He was very aggressive and proactive in his profession as a State Prohibition Agent. James made so many arrests the state could not keep him supplied with enough arrest report forms.

The State of Virginia was only paying James fifty dollars a month for his services while paying other agents in the State one-hundred and twenty-five dollars a month for a much lighter work load. This was not the only dark spot for suitable preparation with James and the State of Virginia as you will soon see.

On December 7th, 1925, Claude F. Beverly wrote a follow up letter to Attorney General John R. Saunders. This letter describes some of the actions by the Dickenson County Sheriff.

It goes as follows: "Dear Mr. Saunders, No let up yet on the part of Sheriff Fleming in trying to drink the county dry.

He was beastly drunk at the Mountain precinct at the recent election and had to be taken care of by friends, to annoyance of women at polling place. This was witnessed by C.S. Colley, Federal Prohibition Agent. A warrant has been issued for him for this.

An indictment was returned by the grand jury at the June, 1921, term of Dickenson court against one Claude M. Fulton, of Norton, for coming into the Clerk's office in the Deckenson temple of Justice on a rip-snorting, hilarious drunk. Indictment was placed in hands of Sheriff Fleming, and he steadily and consistently refused to execute it, notwithstanding the fact that this man Fulton has through all the years since been a frequent business visitor at Clintwood, for the reason that Fleming regarded Fulton (and rightfully so) as a member of the whiskey ring. Finally, the present Commonwealth's Attorney, E.J. Sutherland, had the indictment dismissed, for the reason that he could not get it executed. He told me so. Ex-Commonwealth's Attorney L.N. Sowards, now of Norton, likewise told me that he could never get Sheriff Fleming to execute this indictment. Let this be part of the charges against the Sheriff.

County Police Officer B.H. Moore, of Clintwood, told me today that he assisted in capturing a young man named Clovis Mullins, who was at that time a U.S. mail carrier, carrying one gallon of whiskey under the mail bags, and that Sheriff Fleming maneuvered this matter around so that Mullins never paid a cent in the way of fine or served a day in jail for the offense.

Commonwealth's Attorney Sutherland told me only a few days ago that the Sheriff and his deputies had reached the point where they would not try to collect a fine off a violator fined by a justice or jury for any offense, that they would make some sort of a shambling return on the capias and turn it in.

On the day of the Democratic primary, last August, Sheriff Fleming and his nephew, A.A. Fleming, engaged in a drunken brawl and fisticuff on the main street at Clintwood in the presence of C.S. Pendleton, Chief Prohibition Agent.

This man has gulped down a gallon of mean fighting booze to where Sheriff Litton, of Washington County, has drank one drop. The outlaws in the county would be in clover, so to speak, were it not for the efforts of a few faithful officers outside his jurisdiction.

Facts as to his conduct are being furnished, and it is hoped by the law-abiding element of the county that this ruffian will be dealt with and not allowed to continue to the end of his term unmolested by ouster proceedings."

Many other citizens including law enforcement officials were complaining on the Sheriff and writing letters in search of Justice.

On January 12th, 1926, County Officer, B.H. Moore wrote a four page letter stating in one paragraph:

"If there is a county in the United States that needs cleaning up, it is Dickenson. Sheriff Fleming has forfeited every right to sympathy. He has betrayed every trust reposed in him by becoming one of the worst violators in the county."

These letters and complaints asking for help raised the ire of Sheriff Pridemore Fleming.

Sheriff Fleming was put on notice by Judge Burns and others that he would be removed from office if he continued drinking and getting in trouble.

The Sheriff started blaming two men for his personal and professional problems, Agent James Mullins and Claude Beverly for his personal problems and the complaints against him, retaliatory threats were made against them both and their families.

Claude F. Beverly was a 1st cousin to Sheriff Pridemore Fleming. Claude Beverly knew from firsthand knowledge what he did not want to catch the ire or wrath from Sheriff Fleming. The Sheriff was very powerful and had friends in high and low places.

Out of desperation, on June 15th, 1926, Claude Beverly wrote a letter requesting Attorney General John Saunders to personally write and inform Sheriff Fleming that a large number of citizens were making complaints against him. It goes as follows:

"Dear Mr. Saunders: Immediately after receipt of enclosed letter I answered and agreed with your idea that it would be better for you to write the Sheriff direct and advise him that statements made by him and some of his deputies to the effect that they were furnished copies of my letters to you about his conduct was and is untrue, and that charge that Prohibition Inspector Mullins and myself were the only ones who made complaint against him was also incorrect. Have never heard a word from you in reply to this matter.

As I have previously advised you, Sheriff Fleming and some of his deputies have stated repeatedly that you furnished them copies of my letters to you about his conduct, and that you advised them that Mr. Mullins and myself were the only ones making complaint to you as to his conduct.

I wished you to write him that a large number of Dickenson county citizens made complaint as to his conduct, because it is dangerous and disagreeable to have a gang of his kind arrayed against you and have to live among them.

Yours Truly, Claude F. Beverly."

The following letter from John H. Saunders, Attorney General to Sheriff Fleming is his attempt to take the heat off of Claude Beverly.

It states the following:

"June 23, 1926, Mr. C.P. Fleming, Freeling, Va. My dear Sir:

I have been informed that you are under the impression that Mr. Claude F. Beverly, of Freeling, Va. is responsible for the charges which were brought against you some time ago in reference to certain violations of the Prohibition Law. In justice to Mr. Beverly I want to state to you that this is a mistake. Before I took this matter up with Judge Skeen and the Commonwealth's Attorney I had on file in my office, and still have, letters from a number of citizens in your County in which complaints were made against you.

I am simply writing this in justice to Mr. Beverly and to disabuse your mind of any erroneous impression which may have been made on you.

I am very much gratified to know that you are keeping your promise to Judge Skeen and I sincerely trust you will continue to do so. With best wishes, I am yours very truly,

John R. Saunders, Attorney General."

The major complication with this letter is that the Attorney General gave cover to Claude Beverly but left James Mullins totally out of the notice. Leaving James out on the limb by himself with a target on this back.

Sometimes it's the little things unsaid or unwritten in this case that have great meaning. Intentionally and / or unintentionally, I believe leaving James Mullins out of this letter planted the seed for the upcoming unfortunate turn of events.

PART SEVEN
DICKENSON AFFAIRS

Born May 6th, 1878, Claudius Pridemore Fleming was the son of William J. Fleming and Mary (Branham) Fleming. He became the Sheriff of Dickenson County in 1920. Pridemore was listed on the 1910 federal census as a farmer and in 1918 as a carpenter for Clinchfields Coal Company.

Pridemore came from a law enforcement family. His brother Tandy Jackson Fleming had served as Sheriff of Dickenson County from 1908-1911.

As a young man Pridemore Fleming made the local Dickenson County newspaper several times before he was to be Sheriff of Dickenson County. The following are newspaper articles describing some of the reported happenings.

"A SHOOTING AFFAIR IN DICKENSON, PRIDEMORE FLEMING PERHAPS FATALLY WOUNDS JAMES WILLIS   DWALE, VA., August 23 (Special) At a gathering in the vicinity of Ava, this county, a day or two since, Pridemore Fleming and James Willis became involved in an altercation, which resulted in the latter being perhaps fatally shot. They first engaged in a fisticuff, but Willis wrenched a large bottle from the hands of one of the bystanders and struck Fleming with it, where-upon Fleming drew a pistol carrying a 18 caliber ball and shot Willis, the bullet taking effect in the left side near the ends of the lower ribs, and ranging towards the backbone.

Dr. Phipps pronounced it a dangerous wound. Fleming surrendered himself to the authorities, and will have a preliminary hearing soon. There seems to be considerable excitement over the affair."

"MAY BE MURDER PRIDEMORE FLEMING SHOOTS JAMES WILLIS - A BOY KILLED   DWALE, VA., Aug. 23 (special) In an altercation between Pridemore Fleming and James Willis, in Ava yesterday, the latter was perhaps fatally shot with a pistol carrying a 18 caliber ball. Fleming at once surrendered himself to the authorities."

"1892 Pridemore FLEMING, the 14 yr. old son of William FLEMING, had the misfortune to have one of his fingers cut off on Saturday."

PART EIGHT
HANDLE IT ACCIDENT

On July 8th 1924, James Mullins reported to his supervisor that he had broken his right arm two days earlier. He was able to attend his circuit court cases during this time. He totally expected that it would only be a month before he would be able to perform moonshine still raiding out in the mountains again without any complications.

Little could be known by James at this time that this minor accident would result in major complications. He would not return home unscathed from this routine trip.

On July 6th, James was on his way to George's Fork to investigate a purported moonshine operation.

He witnessed the beautiful mountains with cascading waterfalls and flat rocks smooth as a baby's skin from years of cool water running over them lying in the creeks concealing the crawdads and other kinds of mountain marine life.

The running creek water blending in with the sounds of the other small animals scurrying through the leaves from around the large rocks protruding from the landscape where "almost heaven" would be an accurate description of the these breath taking views.

James was driving along a dirt road on the side of the mountain not much wider than a wagon trail by and even through the creeks with running waters.

Suddenly, the engine in his T-model Ford automobile popped and backed fired coming to a complete stop on the dirt road. An engine motor stall was not an uncommon occurrence or happenstance while driving around obstacles on the side of a mountain or steep inclines back in 1924.

James got out of the car, grabbed the motor hand crank bar and walked to the front bumper area; he inserted the hand crank bar into the crank port and twisted it.

For some unknown reason the motor back fired while James was attempting to get it started. This motor back fire caused the hand crank bar to quickly kick back in the opposite direction striking him just above the right wrist. This happened so fast, James could not get his hand out of the way in time to avoid hitting his arm. The breaking of the bones would have been as loud as the pop from the motor back firing.

	Not only did this action break his wrist bones but it dislocated the small arm bone all the way up to his right elbow. Completely immobilized, what a dilemma and difficult situation, injured and alone, what to do next? Try to crank the motor again with his left hand with anguishing pain from his right arm, taking another chance that the motor could back fire, or walk to the nearest home which may be miles away.

Either way the next several hours and sudden movements were going to be very painful in a negative breath taking way.

Grease, oil and extra fuel would have been carried in the boot or trunk of these cars. One can be assured that the hand crank bar would have been covered with these fluids making slippage in operation an almost given result.

James was in his late fifties but he was in good health. Much to his disappointment after several weeks he was still experiencing severe pain and swelling up and down his arm. Infection had set into his right arm. With a gut-wrenching injury like this one, I can only surmise that James had his wrist set by a doctor; however this information is not recorded.

After a daily fight with the infection the injury became gangrenous within two months, and before the date of October 4th, James had to have his right arm amputated about one inch and a half above his elbow.

Not missing a beat, James informs his supervisor that he is still working. In fact according to court documents for July 1924 Dickenson County Circuit Court, he had several trials.

Some of the defendants were: Daniel Hay, Earl Short, Gallie Mullins, Ted Baker, Aaron Phipps, Odney Branham, Manning Boggs, Joshua Green, McKinley Mullins, Alex Burk, Alvin Mullins, Pierce Senter and Wiley Hay.

Just weeks after the amputation of his arm the October prohibition docket shows trials with defendants: George Moore, Winston Whestley, Gadrick Mullins, Abraham Salyers, Lefayette Johnson, Eates Fleming, Roy Buckanan, Walter Demron, Harden Robinson, Stuart Rose, George Bryant, Pete Countise, Estes Odle, Worley Smith, Lettie Salyers, Harless Yates, and Albert Stone.

Even though many in the county supported moonshining, these records show that James was hard at work attempting to clear the county of illegal liquor.

James even arrested Estes Fleming for transporting illegal whiskey, he happened to be a cousin to Sheriff Pridemore Fleming.

In fact Estes was married to Oshie Mullins, a cousin to James Mullins. As you can see from the aforesaid mentioned list of names, James was not covering or protecting family members who broke the law either.

PART NINE
COURT HOUSE CONFLICT

As you may know, there has been and will always be bad apples in all professions, including Law Enforcement.

The main focus story of this book starts on a warm summer day on August 6th, 1926. James Mullins had a day trip to Wise County attending to official duties with other Probation Officers. Shortly after returning home to Clintwood he had time to have an early dinner with his wife and children. They ate cornbread and onions. The brown beans hadn't finished cooking yet. No one could know this meal would turn out to be his last meal. James had his dinner early in order to get to the Courthouse before it closed at 5:00 p.m.

He knew that Sheriff Pridemore Fleming had just received his official notice that day informing him of more indictments against him. James must have had a gut feeling that mash wasn't the only thing brewing in the hills of Virginia. Something afoul was afoot, a heaviness from tension like a storm churning in the air. And a large dark storm was brewing!

After many warnings, Sheriff Fleming kept getting into trouble and many people filed complaints against him. Trouble followed him around like a magnet. Trouble seemed like it was his constant companion. E.J. Sutherland informed Attorney General John R. Saunders that he was turning over Sheriff Fleming's resignation paperwork to Judge Burns because of these violations.

The soon to be ex-Sheriff Fleming had been accused of personally violating Prohibition Laws and protecting other moonshiners. Along with a half dozen other criminal offenses.

James Mullins in his official duties took the lead role in obtaining warrants for violations of the prohibition laws. And had been instrumental in having Sheriff Fleming removed from office.

Not long after he arrived, about 5:15 p.m. Inspector James Mullins was sitting on the stone wall above the side walk outside the Dickenson County courthouse discussing a warrant on a Mr. Sydney Colley with colleagues E.J. Sutherland, the Commonwealth's Attorney for Dickenson County, and Miles Sykes, the Justice of the Peace.

These men were discussing pressing business of the State. Officers didn't have set hours or a 9:00 a.m. to 5:00 p.m. job. If you are checking on warrants and talking with your co-workers at the County Courthouse you are on official duty. They asked Justice of the Peace, C.J. Mullins to join in on the discussion as he was leaving the courthouse. It was a common practice for these men to meet near the side wall of the courthouse square each day, weather permitting.

Unembarrassed, but by his red face it was very obvious to the group that he had received his notice. This was their first sign of trouble. The ex-Sheriff stormed by the group of men on his way to the boarding house / hotel that he and his wife operated just down the street from the courthouse.

After about a ten minute discussion on the process of the warrant on Mr. Colley by this group of men, dignity quickly turned to demise.

Ex-Sheriff Fleming, with a hardened heart and an open and ruffled brow, stormed out of the hotel and headed toward the group of men. The group of men were about to break up and take their leave. Unbeknownst to the men, this pass he had his revolver in his hand and vengeance on his mind.

This was the next and last sign of trouble. E.J. Sutherland was the first to see him coming. He noticed a change in the sheriff's demeanor; he could see that he was unstrung and very upset.

E.J. Sutherland caught hold of the ex-Sheriff by the arm in attempt to talk him down some. This attempt was in vain with a voice expressive of his disappointment. The ex-Sheriff was a much larger and stronger man, immersed with tremendous strength; he simply brushed E.J. Sutherland aside.

With a burning in his throat and a tone of resentment, Fleming splintered the quiet surroundings when he ordered the men to "scatter out"; he told them to "get away." And like a Lion eyeing its prey, he zoned in on one man, and that man was James Mullins!

With eager speed he hastened his steps toward James. He raised his revolver and fired the first shot, hitting the ground directly in front of James Mullins.

His heart jumping into his mouth and with a surge of adrenaline, James started to hurriedly back up and stated "don't do this; you don't know what you are doing."

James wore his gun holster on his right side. The butt of his revolver faced to the front. His holster had slipped toward his back while sitting on the stone wall and became extremely difficult for him to reach with his left hand.

As James reached the steps; Fleming fired again striking James through his arm and on the fourth stair step. Hell bent on killing him he shot James again, this time striking James in the torso area, this shot is believed to have torn through his gun belt into his side.

James was shot three more times as he walked up the steps finally reaching the top. He skittered backward attempting to open the door to the courthouse but staff had already locked up for the evening. He quickly stepped behind one of the thirty-six inch pillars on the porch.

Ex-Sheriff Fleming was now out of ammo and his revolver was empty. Being very intoxicated, believing that James had been killed he mistakenly lowered his weapon, stated "we have done a good days work boys." He turned around and slowly started to walk away from the courthouse. Having no idea if Fleming was reloading his gun or not, overcoming fear while severely wounded, James came out from behind the pillar that he was using for cover. Fighting for his breath, he cross drawled and pulled his pearl handled 38 caliber revolver from his holster.

He lifted the revolver up to his eye site, steadied the revolver on his right arm stub and fired a shot striking Fleming near the middle of his back.

Fleming stumbled and instantly fell to the ground. James proceeded down the steps, down the street and down McClure Ave. James called over to E.J. Sutherland, "Come here, "Li", I'm killed."

At this point two men stopped to assist him into the Sutherland Hospital. These two men were John Powers and Guy Pizzuto.

John Shortt and another man picked up Fleming and carried him to the same Hospital. Both men were basically fighting for their life in the same operating room. When the doctors heard what had happened during the shooting one of them rather indignantly stated, "I can only work on one man at a time, and Inspector Mullins comes first."

Both men were dripping blood onto the operating floor. Ex-Sheriff Fleming succumbed to his wound, about thirty minutes after he arrived.

For the next two days, five different doctors attempted to save James from certain death. Doctors Sutherland, Phipps, Reed, Chalmers and Moore did the best they could under the circumstances.

James had suffered massive loss of blood and this would unfortunately lead to his wounds being fatal. Due to the Doctors valent effects, James lived from the time he was shot on the evening of the 6th, until 1:50 a.m. on the 8th.

Sheriff Fleming was known for violating prohibition laws, and for this reason he and James Mullins had a history of not getting along, it was a professional feud, not a family feud.

Justice of the Peace C.J. Mullins had fined Sheriff Fleming three different times for intoxication. According to E.J. Sutherland's written testimony, Fleming seemed to be under the influence of alcohol during the shootout.

James Mullins had served with the Virginia Prohibition Department for two and a half years. He had previously served as a Dickenson County Deputy, justice of the peace, and as a US Deputy Marshall.

Now widowed, Cordelia Mullins applied for a workers compensation death benefit to help support her family. The state of Virginia denied her request stating the shootout was over a family feud.

Being a fighter also, it was up to Cordelia Mullins to prove to the state that James was killed in the line of duty. From 1926 until 1929 Cordelia Mullins and her attorneys Mesers, Chase & McCoy from Clintwood, Virginia filed their way through the maze of the appeal processes.

On July 22nd, 1929, the Industrial Commission of Virginia in Richmond dismissed the claim by the widow of James Mullins.

They stated she failed to sustain the burden of proving that the death of the deceased was the result of an accident arising out of and in the course of employment. The State once again used the reason of "a feud" to deny his death benefit to Cordelia Mullins.

The records have shown that the benefit was denied due to the fact that a reasonable conclusion about what was going on behind the scene was not proven.

I certainly believe that based on my research a so called family feud had nothing to do with the murder of James Sherman Mullins.

The main reason for no suitable preparations with a workers compensation death benefit for the family of James Mullins was given as follows in the August 26, 1926 letter from Attorney General John R. Saunders to W.B. Phipps, of the Law Offices of Meser, Chase & McCoy:

"Mr. W.B. Phipps, Clintwood, Va.

My dear Sir: I beg leave to acknowledge receipt of your Aug. 23rc, the contents of which I have carefully noted.

I regret to say that this Department has no insurance on its employees. When I first took charge of the enforcement of prohibition, Sept., 1922, I at once insured every man who was employed in the Department.

For nearly three years this insurance was kept inforce but so many casualties occurred, the companies declined to write insurance and for more than a year I have been unable to get compensation insurance for the men though I have tried to do this in a number of companies; this, of course, was not my fault.

Should it be decided that Mrs. Mullins is entitled to compensation; the only way she could obtain it would be by an act of the Legislature making an appropriation for her. Of course, I have the deepest sympathy for Mrs. Mullins and her children.

Yours very Truly, John R. Saunders, Attorney General. "

As we can plainly see the Industrial Commission had no intention of awarding a benefit to the Mullins family from the start. The State of Virginia did not have insurance in place to cover Agents killed in the line of duty.

Attorney General John R. Saunders must have had somewhat of an attack on his conscience; on September 16th, 1926 he mailed a check to Cordelia Mullins for the sum of $12.50. This was pay for James Mullins working the first week of August before he was killed. He had to have known that would be the last sum of pay Cordelia Mullins and her children would ever receive from the State of Virginia.

James was survived by his wife and thirteen children, Cordelia still had three children at home and she had no income.

Unfortunately, sympathy doesn't put food on the table or pay the bills for a widow and children. Cordelia Mullins had to travel by horse selling fruits and vegetables she could grow to make ends meet.

Life was difficult for James's family because authorities called the gun fight a family feud; Cordelia never received the workers compensation pension or death funds that should have been in place for officers shot in the line of duty.

The final workers compensation pension appeal denial could not have come at a worst time.

The Great Depression hit our country in 1929 with devastating economic impact. Over the next four years the unemployment rate increased to 24.9%. It was almost impossible to find a new job. Cordelia, now in her sixties was almost unemployable. Even young and health men and women couldn't find work.

Police Chief Levi Hall from Splash Dam Virginia was appointed Sheriff of Dickenson County by Judge Burns on August 25th, 1926. B.H. Moore of Clintwood was the applicant for the position of State Prohibition Agent held by the late James Sherman Mullins.

The State of Virginia failed to recognize that James Mullins was killed in the line of duty for eighty-six years. Thanks to the hard work and research of his granddaughter, Jenny Cooper, James S. Mullins is now in the National Law Enforcement Officer's Memorial in Washington, D.C.

His name is included at the memorial among 19,000 other officers who died in the line of duty.

PART TEN

WRIGHT FAMILY

We have all heard good and bad stories about John W. "Devil John" Wright as a Wise County Sheriff and a Letcher County U.S. Marshall. Most have not heard about the suspicious and mysterious shooting involving his brother Samuel Wright who at the time of his death was a Neon Town Police Officer. Good cop or bad cop during this time in history the Wright families in the Cumberland Mountain Range area carried a heavy burden with losses in the Law Enforcement community.

Several of Deputy Constable Joel Martin Wright's second cousins were shot and killed in the line of duty while serving as law enforcement officers in Letcher County, Kentucky.

Along with Deputy Joel Martin Wright, Letcher County Sheriff's Deputy William S. Wright was shot and killed on Tuesday, January 30th, 1900. Deputy William Wright was shot and killed from ambush by two members of the Ku Klux Klan.

Deputy Wright was targeted because of his involvement with quelling a Klan war that had erupted in Letcher County. He had also assisted with protecting a woman and her son who had been beaten and robbed by members of the Ku Klux Klan.

Both suspects were arrested and convicted of his murder and sentenced to life in prison. Deputy William Wright had served with the agency for only three months. He was survived by his wife Letitia (Bates) Wright and eleven children.

Less than a year and a half later, his son, Deputy William S. Wright Jr. was shot on April 9th, and died on April 10th, 1901, while serving in the line of duty with the Letcher County Sheriff's Department.

Deputy William Wright Jr. was shot and killed when he and his partner were ambushed. The two deputies were in route to serve murder warrants on two suspects when the suspects ambushed them.

Deputy William Wright Jr. was mortally wounded and died the next day. The other officer survived the shooting. Both suspects were eventually apprehended and charged with Deputy Wright's murder. William was only Eighteen-years-old and had been with the agency for four months at the time of his murder.

Just seven weeks before the shooting between Pridmore Fleming and James S. Mullins there was another illegal alcohol related shooting. On June 13th, 1926 Letcher County Deputy Sheriff James Robert "Bob" Wright was shot and killed as he, Sheriff Morgan T. Reynolds, Prohibition Officer Clark Day, and several other deputies served a search warrant at a boarding house in Burdine, Kentucky. The boarding house was being operated by Joe Centi. This boarding house was known for making and selling illegal wine.

The officers arrived at the house shortly after midnight and announced that they had a warrant. The occupants refused to let them enter and demanded they leave. After several minutes the officers entered the lower level of the home while the occupants remained on the top level.

Upon finding three large kegs / containers of wine Prohibition Officer Clark Day and Deputy James R. Wright started to go up the stairs to arrest the suspects. As they did one of the men opened fire from a side room, striking Deputy James R. Wright. He was taken to a local hospital where he died approximately thirty minutes later.

The suspect Joe Vignioroto who shot Deputy James R. Wright was arrested without further incident. Both men were transported to a jail in a neighboring county for their own safety.

The Mountain Eagle Press Newspaper listed two suspects involved in the shooting; Joe Vignioroto and Joe Centi. Joe Vignioroto was tried and convicted of murder; he served fifteen years in the State Penitentiary.

Deputy James R. Wright had served with the Letcher County Sheriff's Office for only two months. He was survived by his wife Anne (Wallen) Wright and five children.

Deputy Constable Booker V. Wright was shot and killed on November 7th, 1932, while serving with the Letcher County Constable's Office. Deputy Constable Wright was shot when he went to a house to arrest a suspect on a warrant with an officer from the Neon Police Department.

When Deputy Constable Wright arrived at the suspect's home to serve a warrant for public intoxication, the suspect opened fire on the officers. Deputy Constable Wright was able to return fire, but was struck in both thighs which severed an artery in one leg.

The suspect was arrested by the other Town of Neon officer and charged with murder. He was found not guilty by reason of self-defense. This suspect may have believed that someone was attempting to break into his home.

Booker V. Wright was survived by his wife and three children.

CONCLUSION

The Mullins and Fleming families were early pioneers of Virginia and Kentucky. They were people of incredible independence. Their independence helped tamed the wilderness during that time.

Like the stories with the Hatfields and McCoys, John "Devil John" Wright was both a lawman and an outlaw; Marshall Benton "Doc" Taylor was both a lawman and an outlaw. We have the same circumstances with the Fleming and Mullins families; they have had their good and their bad, their ups and their downs. We know that these families are true Americans, Patriotic and God fearing. Stories such as these keep our family trees busy and ablaze with the folklore and tales of the old days.

History documents the fruit of the vine being used to make strong drink. Like the forbidden fruit in the Garden of Eden, Adam and Eve ate of the fruit of the tree for knowledge of the mind. Since then man has been very creative and has used fruits to ferment and make spiritual liquors to alter the mind.

I personally believe that excess of any substances is not good for the soul. The King James Version of the Holy Bible states in Ephesians 5: 18 "And be not drunk with wine, wherein is excess; but be filled with the Spirit."

From my life experiences, only bad things come from excess. The irony of too much liquor is reminiscent of the story in which God punished the serpent to crawl on his belly for the rest of his days for deceiving Adam and Eve.

Man is still listening to the serpent and allowing himself to be brought down to the serpent's ground level with drunkenness from the same fruit of the tree and vines. We were given fruits for nourishment, the enemy's plan is to cloud God's purposes and leave us to wander aimlessly about in a fog of confusion and drunkenness. Ultimately this leads us to addiction and discouragement, all the wiles of Satan.

Family history is far better than the fiction we see on television now a days and its far more interesting wouldn't you say? You can't make this kind of stuff up.

On a side note, E.J. Sutherland's great uncle was Capt. Ezekiel "Zeke" Counts through his mother Eliza Jane Counts. He is infamous in my book "Deadman's Hollow," another true story about Dickenson County affairs.

SOURCES

According to recorded official eyewitness Statements

The Historical Society of the Pound, Pound, Virginia

The Historical Society of Dickenson County, Virginia

Newspaper the Tribune Herald

The Rome Tribune Herald Newspaper November 8th, 1914

Sworn affidavit by Sidney Tackett dated September 8th, 1915

The Big Sandy News, September 10th, 1915

Washington Star, Evening News, February 15th, 1922

Ancestry.com Family Records

Mountain Eagle Newspaper, Whitesburg, Letcher County, Kentucky, Thursday, June 17, 1926

Holy Bible - Ephesians 5: 18

Carnage In Clintwood

Personal information from Jennie Cooper, Granddaughter of James S. Mullins

ACKNOWLEDGMENTS

To my wife and Co-Author Doris Gail (Barber) Baldwin, whose love and giving support make all things possible. A true Proverbs 31: 10-31 wife.

To my son Roy Dean Baldwin, and my daughter Amanda C. Baldwin, many thanks for your long hours and hard work.

A special thanks to Jennie Cooper for her research with her grandfather James S. Mullins. The holster on the cover is the actual holster worn by James S. Mullins during his murder. Upon inspection you can see a bullet hole in the belt above the holster. The back cover is a picture of James S. Mullins and wife Cordelia.

Friend me at Facebook page:

https://www.facebook.com/The-Baldwin-Stories

Please remember to write an online review. Thank you.

Contact email:
thebaldwinstories@gmail.com

Check out my other stories and books at:

http://thebaldwinstories.wix.com/author-blog

Made in the USA
Monee, IL
15 June 2020

33536828R00075